Loving Well

BETH MOORE

LifeWay Press®
Nashville, TN

Published by LifeWay Press®
© 2007 • Beth Moore
Reprinted 2015

ISBN 978-1-4158-2594-5
Item 001310905

Dewey Decimal classification: 248.843
Subject headings: WOMEN \ CHRISTIAN LIFE \ STRESS (PSYCHOLOGY)

Cover design by The DesignWorks Group
Interior design by Susan Browne Design

Unless otherwise noted, all Scripture quotations are taken from the Holman Christian Standard Bible®, copyright © 1999, 2000, 2001, 2002, 2003 by Holman Bible Publishers. Used by permission. Scripture quotations identified AMP are taken from The Amplified® Bible, copyright © 1954, 1958, 1962, 1964, 1965, 1987 by the Lockman Foundation. Used by permission. *(www. lockman.org)*. Scripture quotations identified NIV are taken from The New International Version © International Bible Publishers 1973, 1978, 1984. Used by permission.

To order additional copies of this resource: write LifeWay Church Resources Customer Service; One LifeWay Plaza; Nashville, TN 37234-0113; fax 615.251.5933; phone toll free 800.458.2772; order online at *www.lifeway.com;* email *orderentry@lifeway.com;* or visit the LifeWay Christian Store serving you.

Printed in the United States of America

Adult Ministry Publishing
LifeWay Church Resources
One LifeWay Plaza
Nashville, TN 37234-0152

Dedication

To Carolyn O'Neal,

How can I ever think of women's ministry and all manner of women's retreats without thinking of you? You are one of the most gracious servants of God I've ever known. I have been deeply impacted by your devoted ministry to women of all ages at our church. I am among the many in our congregation who love you dearly. Keep doing what you do, my dear friend. Jesus is worthy!

I love and respect you so much,

Beth

About Beth Moore

Beth Moore realized at the age of 18 that God was claiming her future for full-time ministry. While she was sponsoring a cabin of sixth-graders at a missions camp, God unmistakably acknowledged that she would work for Him. There Beth conceded all rights to the Lord she had loved since childhood. However, she encountered a problem: Although she knew she was "wonderfully made," she was "fearfully" without talent.

Beth hid behind closed doors to discover whether a beautiful singing voice had miraculously developed, but the results were tragic. She returned to the piano from which years of fruitless practice had streamed but found the noise to be joyless. Finally accepting that the only remaining alternative was missions work in a foreign country, she struck a martyr's pose and waited. Yet nothing happened.

Still confident of God's calling, Beth finished her degree at Southwest Texas State University, where she fell in love with Keith. After they married in December 1978, God added daughters Amanda and Melissa to their household.

As if putting together puzzle pieces one at a time, God filled Beth's path with supportive persons who saw something in her she could not. God used individuals such as Marge Caldwell, John Bisagno, and Jeannette Cliff George to help Beth discover gifts of speaking, teaching, and writing. Seventeen years after her first speaking engagement, those gifts have spread all over the nation. Her joy and excitement in Christ are contagious; her deep love for the Savior, obvious; her style of speaking, electric.

Beth and her husband, Keith, are devoted to the local church and have the privilege of attending Bayou City Fellowship in Houston, Texas, where their son-in-law Curtis Jones pastors. Beth believes that her calling is Bible literacy: guiding believers to love and live God's Word. Beth has a passion for Christ, a passion for Bible study, and a passion to see Christians living the lives Christ intended.

Beth loves the Lord, loves to laugh, and loves to be with His people. Her life is full of activity, but one commitment remains constant: counting all things but loss for the excellence of knowing Christ Jesus, the Lord (see Phil. 3:8).

Beth's previous Bible studies have explored the lives of Moses, David, Paul, Isaiah, Daniel, and Jesus. In *Loving Well* she invites you along to allow God to love you well and then to love others. May you be blessed by your journey, as were those who traveled to Knoxville for the retreat and those who worked with Beth to bring you *Loving Well*.

Introduction

Welcome to *Loving Well*. I'm so delighted that you have chosen to join us in this study of what is both a core challenge and a central joy of following Christ. We're going to jump into the Word to seek help in loving all the people God has for us.

You probably remember those old commercials where two people collided: "You got chocolate in my peanut butter," and "You got peanut butter in my chocolate." Well, in the fall of 2005 God brought several things together that resulted in *Loving Well*.

At that time, the Living Proof Live event team was preparing for what was going to be a special occasion. We were going for a weekend to Knoxville, Tennessee, and we sensed that God was up to something.

God had been dealing with me about loving people. He kept bringing me back to 1 John 4:7-8. As I prepared, God spoke to me about the four kinds of people we studied that weekend. Some are easy to love. Some are difficult to love, and some are humanly impossible to love. God wants to demonstrate His

might by doing through us what we cannot possibly do on our own. He wants us to learn to love all of these kinds of people—and love them well. So in Knoxville God spoke to us about the only way we can love well—with His love providing the key to how we can love them.

At the same time God was speaking to me about loving well, He was doing a new thing with my friends at LifeWay. We have done more than 80 Living Proof Live events together. We had never sought to capture any of them on video, but for the Knoxville event LifeWay sent a video crew.

No good collision around the Moore house could only involve two parties, though, so God brought in a third part of it all. For a couple of years people had been asking for something to help churches conduct a weekend retreat. We realized that the Knoxville weekend would be a great time to invite friends from all over to participate.

Now those of you who know me know that nothing would please

me more than to run off to some secluded spot and spend time with you in the Word. I want to sit and talk like the girlfriends we have become. We may have to wait for heaven to ultimately sit down together for that kind of personal sharing, but I hope *Loving Well* can be at least a taste of it for both of us. I'm not kidding when I tell you that you've become my dear friends though we've only gotten to study God's Word together through the page and video.

The LifeWay team has taken the time at Knoxville and formatted it for a weekend retreat. Or you may choose to study *Loving Well* in a four-week video study. My friend Julie Woodruff has written plans to prepare and conduct the retreat. My buddy Travis Cottrell has provided helps for worship leaders. And then Travis and I got together to provide some fun things you'll find on the DVD menus. I hope you have as much fun with it all as we have.

This journal is not a study in the normal sense. In Knoxville, God really spoke to us about loving well.

I wanted us to have some time to reflect on and apply the teaching. So this journal takes the content of the video and invites you to spend time with the Father. I want you to have a chance to personalize and apply the concepts.

If you use *Loving Well* in a retreat, the journal gives you four weeks of follow up. If you choose to take the four-week study approach, the journal will allow you to reflect on the time together each week. I hope it will be an enriching time with you, your Bible, and the Lord. Then one day you can brew me a cup of coffee and tell me how He loved you well.

I love you,

Beth Moore

LOVE SPRINGS FROM GOD

Drawing from the Well

"Beloved, let us love one another, for love is [springs] from God and he who loves [his fellowmen] is begotten [born] of God and is coming [progressively] to know and understand God [to perceive and recognize and get a better and clearer knowledge of Him]."
1 John 4:7, AMP

We use the word *love* glibly, "I love my husband, I love my children, I love my grandbaby, I love my dog, I love coffee, and I love Mexican food." You get the idea. But we need to ask ourselves what it means to love well.

I'm convinced that to love well requires a persevering love that goes beyond our human capabilities. We cannot love well unless we have a growing personal relationship with Christ. If we are growing in Christ, we are growing in love because "love springs from God." We have no higher calling than to love. God measures maturity by how we love.

Over the next four weeks we want to evaluate the way we love others. Let's begin by asking ourselves some questions. Take a moment to journal your thoughts in response to the following questions:

Do I love others better than I did five years ago?

Week One • Learning to Love

Am I growing in my ability to love others more openly, with more vulnerability?

_____

_____

_____

_____

_____

_____

What marked change or transformation has come about in the way I love?

_____

_____

_____

_____

_____

_____

_____

_____

_____

As you ponder these questions today, ask God to show you where you can grow in love.

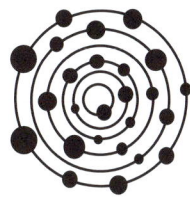 **PRAYER** Father, thank You for loving me and demonstrating that love by sending Jesus to die on the cross for my sins. Teach me to love others well by giving of myself—even beyond what I am capable. Thank You that I can do that because love comes from You.

GOD'S LOVE

Drawing from the Well

"This is how God showed his love among us: He sent his one and only Son into the world that we might live through him. This is love: not that we loved God, but that he loved us and sent his Son as an atoning sacrifice for our sins. Dear friends, since God so loved us, we also ought to love one another. No one has ever seen God; but if we love one another, God lives in us and his love is made complete in us." *1 John 4:9-12, NIV*

Our goal is not just to learn to love but also to grow in our capacity to love well. No one has ever seen God, but when we love beyond our abilities, people will see Him in us. More than our teaching, serving, or exhorting, God manifests Himself through us when we love.

Today's verse, "This is love: not that we loved God, but that he loved us" sounds easy. But part of the problem we have in learning to love others is that we don't take time to let God minister to and love on us.

When was the last time you confessed to God that you need to bask in His love before you can love others? Unless He fills us with love, we will be unable to pour out God's love on others.

Read 1 John 4:7-17 and write down everything these verses have to say about love.

Do you really believe God loves you? Why or why not?

Carve out some time today or this week to spend an extended time alone with God. Go to a quiet place, taking only your Bible and your journal.

Talk with God about any fears or doubts you might have. Ask Him to show you His love today.

PRAYER Father, I confess that sometimes I try to love others out of a sense of duty rather than out of a heart that overflows with Your love. I have been reminded that I cannot give to others what I have not received. Before I can love anybody else, I need You to love me.

COLD LOVE

Drawing from the Well

"The love of most will grow cold." Matthew 24:12, NIV

The closer we come to Christ's return, the more our world will be characterized by two very scary things: The love of many will grow cold, and people will be characterized by self-love. It is imperative that we keep reminding ourselves as the people of God that we're called to love. Let's consider why the love of many will grow cold.

We can easily become desensitized through total overexposure to violence and peril. So much heartache surrounds us that we defend ourselves by binding up our own hearts just so we can stand it. As we do that, we find our hearts growing cold.

We also develop cold hearts because we try to bind up our own wounds rather than letting God heal us. What many of us do when we try to bind up our own wounds is put duct tape around them. After all, duct tape is supposed to hold anything in place. The problem is duct tape doesn't work on a broken heart. We must allow God to heal our hearts from the inside out.

In what ways have you been hurt so that you tried to bind up your heart with duct tape?

Have you asked God to heal your heart from the inside out to keep you from becoming hardened and so your love will not grow cold?

In what areas do you need God's touch today?

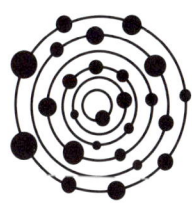

PRAYER Father, I realize that the only way my heart can be healed is if I allow You to heal it. I ask You to protect me from allowing my heart to grow cold. Help me to strip off any duct tape I've used to bind my broken heart and to allow You to heal me and set me free.

4

SELF-LOVE

Drawing from the Well

"But know this: difficult times will come in the last days. For people will be lovers of self, lovers of money, boastful, proud, blasphemers, disobedient to parents, ungrateful, unholy, unloving, irreconcilable, slanderers, without self-control, brutal, without love for what is good, traitors, reckless, conceited, lovers of pleasure rather than lovers of God, holding to the form of religion but denying its power." *2 Timothy 3:1-5, HCSB*

Yesterday we discussed one reason to remember our call to love—so our hearts won't grow cold. Today consider another. In the last days people will be characterized by self-love. Everything that surrounds us—the media, the covers of magazines—begs us to love self.

Remember the Greek word for *self-love* we learned in the video? It included "an undue sparing of self, with the primary concern that things be easy and pleasant for one's self." Here's what we'll do if we aren't careful: We will spare ourselves the effort because loving people will always involve risk and always mean they have access to hurt us. We'll cease relating on the heart level and start relating on the verbal level. We talk it; we just don't do it because we can get hurt. Beloved, we must risk getting hurt if we are going to have deep relationships. Any relationship worth having is worth going deep, hurt and all.

"There is no fear in love; instead, perfect love drives out fear" (1 John 4:18). When we allow God to love us first, He frees us to love others well.

Have you avoided some potentially healthy relationship because you were afraid of getting hurt?

What happens when you refuse to allow people access to your heart?

....
....
....
....
....
....
....
....
....

What positive changes might result if you allow God complete access to your heart?

....
....
....
....
....
....
....
....
....
....
....

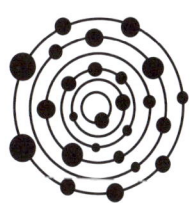 **PRAYER** Lord, I have missed out on some relationships fearing I would be hurt. Help me to risk going deep to find the joy that comes from relating on a heart level.

RECOGNIZING GOD'S LOVE

Drawing from the Well

"We know that we live in him and he in us, because he has given us of his Spirit. And we have seen and testify that the Father has sent his Son to be the Savior of the world. If anyone acknowledges that Jesus is the Son of God, God lives in him and he in God. And so we know and rely on the love God has for us."
1 John 4:13-16, NIV

We must allow God to minister His love to us because we will never learn to love well without letting Him love us well. The Amplified version of 1 John 4:16 reads, "We know [understand, recognize, are conscious of, by observation and by experience] and believe [adhere to and put faith in and rely on] the love God cherishes for us." When God shows His love to us, we recognize it. Are you able to recognize God's love for you, or has all you've been through blinded you to His love? We must ask God to heal our spiritual sight so we can recognize His love for us.

I pray that we will become persons who don't just know about His love in our heads. I pray that we experience His love emotionally as well as spiritually. I pray that we feel Him way down in our spiritual gut—know God completely loves and cherishes us. If He does not get through to us, we will be unhealthy believers all our lives.

Do you know that God completely loves and cherishes you?

Week One • Learning to Love

How have you experienced His love?

How are you seeking to experience His love today?

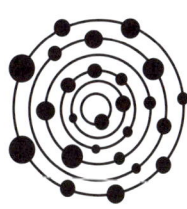 **PRAYER** Thank You, Lord, that I know in my head that You love me. However, I understand there is so much more to knowing the love of God. I don't want to settle for just knowing intellectually that You love me. I want to know Your love by experiencing it.

WEEK IN REVIEW

This week we have focused on learning to love well. What new truths from God's Word have you learned about loving well?

What fears do you have about developing deep relationships?

Is allowing God to love on you a difficult thing? If so, why?

Which people have come to your mind this week as you have been learning what it means to love well? List their names below. Pray that God would give you courage and boldness to love them well. Write out your prayer beneath the names you list.

WEEK IN REVIEW

Let's apply what we have learned this week. List below some actions you can take to love well those in your life. Some suggestions might be to write a note of encouragement, make a phone call, make arrangements to get together for a cup of coffee, and so forth.

Week One • Learning to Love

PRAYER Lord, I confess that I have used the word *love* flippantly on many occasions. I understand that love comes from You. Help me this week to love others well not just by speaking it but by demonstrating my love to them.

FOUR CONFESSIONS OF LOVE

Drawing from the Well

"God is love." *1 John 4:8,16*

"There is no fear in love; instead, perfect love drives out fear."
1 John 4:18

The four confessions of love help us with the challenge to love others. As you memorize these confessions and remind yourself of them, I believe they will radically transform the way you love others. Each time you encounter a challenge to love someone, go through these confessions in your mind.

Spend time memorizing these four confessions. As we learn what it means to love well, these concepts will become very important to us. My prayer is that these confessions become so ingrained in your heart and mind that years from now you will remember them when you are challenged to love a difficult person.

Journal your thoughts about each of these confessions:

1. God is perfect love (1 John 4:18).

2. Nothing can separate me from God's perfect love (Rom. 8:38-39).

_____
_____
_____
_____

3. God pours His perfect love into my imperfect heart (Rom. 5:5).

_____
_____
_____
_____

4. Accessed, I can love anyone through anything (Phil. 4:13).

_____
_____
_____
_____

 **PRAYER** God, thank You that Your love is perfect and that nothing can separate me from Your perfect love. Thank You for pouring Your perfect love into my imperfect heart. Help me to remember that when I access those first three confessions, then I can love anyone through anything.

WE LOVE BECAUSE HE FIRST LOVED US

Drawing from the Well

"We love because He first loved us. If anyone says, 'I love God,' yet hates his brother, he is a liar. For the person who does not love his brother whom he has seen cannot love God whom he has not seen." *1 John 4:19-20*

See if you can write the confessions from memory. I'll give you some help:

1. God is _____ love.

2. _____ can _____ me from God's perfect love.

3. God _____ His _____ love into my _____ heart.

4. _____, I can love _____ through anything.

Great job.

Do you love some people because you need someone to love you? Human love even at its best is self-seeking. If we don't have some divine love pouring through us, we will love as a means of getting love in return.

Our human tendency is to think about what we can get out of a relationship. However, God empowers us to love others because we have been loved by Him.

Not only do we love God because He first loved us, but we can love others because God first loved us. When we understand how much we are loved, we are freed to love anyone. What a difference it would make if we were motivated to love others by something other than our own desire for someone to love us.

The writer of Proverbs said that what a man craves most is unfailing love. When we continually look for unfailing love in humans, we are never satisfied. Let's learn to get our hearts filled up by the love of God rather than seeking it from other people. For us to be healthy, whole persons who love, we must first understand that God unfailingly, steadfastly, and perfectly loves us.

How do you feel when you realize that someone's love for you is motivated by his or her desire to be loved?

What difference does it make for your love to be motivated by God's love for you?

How do you feel about God's unfailing, perfect love for you?

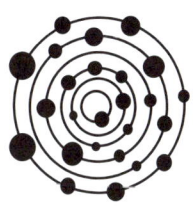 **PRAYER** I confess that I have been guilty of loving others so that they would love me in return. My desire is to be free to love others because my heart has been filled up by Your unfailing, perfect love.

THE FRUIT OF THE SPIRIT IS LOVE

Drawing from the Well

"The fruit of the Spirit is love." *Galatians 5:22*

Do you remember the confessions? See if you can write them below. No peeking ... Oh OK, if you have to, but try to do it without looking back.

Let's consider the first confession again: *God is perfect love.* If God is love, then love is not just a feeling to God. It cannot be changed by a circumstance or displaced by anger, judgment, or anything else. For example, I am a woman. It doesn't matter what I do or what I feel, I am still woman. I've gotten letters from precious women who have had mastectomies or hysterectomies, but I am telling you that there is no surgery on earth that can make you less of a woman. You are just woman!

God is love. That is who He is. Since God is love, when He fills us with His Holy Spirit, what is the first fruit that is produced in us? When the Holy Spirit fills us, we are filled with the Spirit of Christ Himself, so we are filled with love. Love is part of God's goodness. Therefore, nothing you or I can do will make God love us any less—love is not an emotion to God. It is an expression of His goodness. We love as an emotion, but Christ through us displays the divine love of God.

Week Two • God's Perfect Love

How do you feel when you consider the constant nature of God's love?

Why is our love so much less constant than God's?

What difference can reminding yourself of God's love make in your life?

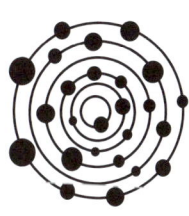 **PRAYER** I praise You because You are love. So many times love is just a feeling to me. I thank You that love is more than a feeling to You; it is Your very character. Help me to love others not in my natural self but rather my supernatural self.

FEARLESS LOVE

Drawing from the Well

"There is no fear in love. But perfect love drives out fear, because fear has to do with punishment." *1 John 4:18*

Perfect love means a love that is complete. In the Greek, the word is *teleios*. Not only does it mean "complete" but it also means "to reach its goal." God's love is complete in us and complete to us.

Read verse 18 again. What drives out fear? _____ _____

The one who fears is not made perfect in love. In other words, when we stay in a state of fear, we are not letting God's love accomplish its goal in us.

The rest of the definition for *teleios* reads, "Perfect love refers to love which is mature, not lacking boldness or confidence and therefore, not hampered by insecurity or anxiety which is characteristic of immature love." This is one way we know if we're really letting God love us with His love. There's no question He loves us, but are we allowing Him to appropriate His love to us? To the degree that we battle insecurity and anxiety, we are not letting the love of God reach its goal in our hearts.

On a scale of 1 to 10, 1 being completely secure and 10 being completely insecure, where would you find yourself?

1   2   3   4   5   6   7   8   9   10

completely secure   completely insecure

What situations particularly expose your insecurities?

....

....

....

....

How can you allow God's love to minister to you in those situations?

....

....

....

....

We'll discuss this more tomorrow. Until then, take some time to evaluate your insecurities and anxieties. List those things you struggle with.

....

....

....

....

PRAYER Lord, I confess that I struggle with insecurity and anxiety. Today I have learned that I am not allowing You to love me with Your perfect love when I am in a state of fear. Help me to deal with these areas in my life so that Your perfect love can drive out the fear in me.

NOTHING CAN SEPARATE

Drawing from the Well

"For I am persuaded that neither death nor life, nor angels nor rulers, nor things present, nor things to come, nor powers, nor height, nor depth, nor any other created thing will have the power to separate us from the love of God that is in Christ Jesus our Lord!" *Romans 8:38-39*

Let's continue today where we left off yesterday. I have dealt with insecurity all my life for a thousand different reasons. Every insecurity that you could possibly have, I've dealt with too. When I am in my natural self, I still deal with it.

We have got to get to the root of this. God's Word says that we are not yet mature in love—not how we love, but how we allow God to love us—if we are fraught with insecurity. It is the outgrowth of unbelief. No matter how we dress it and try to make it look like humility, it is unbelief. Its root is pride.

Remember confession number two?

_____ *can* _____ *us from God's perfect love.*

Your anger can't separate you from the love of God. Your sin, hatred, your self-righteousness, your stronghold, your addiction, the Devil himself cannot separate you from the love of God. His love to us is unlike anybody else's love will ever be to us.

Read the following questions and statements I believe God wants to ask or say to you. Just revel in His love for you.

1. Do you realize that I came to meet with you?

2. Do you have any idea how much I love you? How taken I am with you?

3. Do you know that I have never forsaken you nor will I ever reject you? I was there all along. I always will be.

4. Do you realize I knew everything about you the day you were conceived? I anticipated your life and planned for it.

5. You do have an enemy, My Child. But it is not Me. He wants you to think it is.

6. I am for you.

7. Do you think you need to prove yourself lovable to Me? Deep down inside, are you trying to earn My love and attention?

8. As you strive to love Me more, do you realize the key to loving Me more is to let Me love you more?

9. Why are you resisting Me? Why are you running from Me?

10. To whom have you compared Me, and with whom have you confused Me?

11. I'm not like them.

12. I know what's happened. I know what's on your mind.

13. I alone know the plan for how this turns out well. I alone know how to prosper you through this.

14. My eyes and My affections are on you right now.

15. Quit trying to be so strong. Let Me be strong for you.

16. I love you unashamedly. Even now My banner flies over you. Everyone in the heavenlies knows how I feel about you. I'd leave you red-faced over My love for you … if you'd let Me.

 **PRAYER** Thank You, Lord, that nothing can separate me from Your love. I rejoice today that Your love for me is perfect. There is no one like You. I love You.

WEEK
IN REVIEW

This week we have focused on God's perfect love. What new truths have you learned from God's Word about His perfect love?

Based on what you have learned this week, what does "perfect love" mean?

In what ways has God shown His perfect love toward you?

What are some hindrances that keep you from accepting God's perfect love?

Week Two • God's Perfect Love

What statements from day 5 ministered to you most? Why?

Write a prayer below expressing your gratitude to God for His perfect love.

WEEK
IN REVIEW

Write below the four confessions
that we learned this week.

How can these confessions radically transform
the way you love others?

What are some relationships in your life where
you need to access God's perfect love in order to
love those people well?

What do you need to do this week to access God's perfect love in your life?

Lord, help me to remember this week as I deal with people in my life that You are perfect love and that nothing can separate me from Your perfect love. Thank You for pouring Your perfect love into my imperfect heart. When I am challenged to love someone, remind me that I can access Your perfect love and love anyone through anything.

JOY

Drawing from the Well

"Therefore, my brothers, you whom I love and long for, my joy and crown." *Philippians 4:1, NIV*

This week we are going to review the four kinds of people we love or are challenged to love. Remember? We named them *Joy*, *Testy*, *Foe*, and *Far*. Each of these names describes people we are challenged to love. Thankfully, God never calls us to do something He doesn't also empower us to do. Because His Spirit lives in us, we have the power to love beyond ourselves.

Today we want to consider the people who are a joy to love. Think about the people who bring you joy. Maybe it's someone in your family, a friend, someone from church, a child, or an older person.

Aren't you thankful for the people who bring you joy? They don't have to be perfect or never create conflict. You can honestly say those people are just a joy to love. You love spending time with them, and when you do, time seems to fly.

As you think about the people who are a joy to love, what is it about them that brings you joy?

Week Three • Loving People

What about you? How do you bring joy to others?

....

....

....

....

....

....

....

....

....

....

Take a moment to write a card or call those people who are a joy to love and tell them what they mean to you.

....

....

....

....

....

....

....

....

....

....

....

....

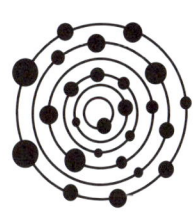

PRAYER Lord, thank You for the people in my life who are a pure joy to love. Help me to bring joy to others.

TESTY

Drawing from the Well

"I urge Euodia and I urge Syntyche to agree in the Lord."

Philippians 4:2

After Paul rejoiced over those he loved in Philippians 4:1, his next words were to encourage two women to get along! Testy is probably the biggest problem in our relational world. Testy is the person who drives you crazy. When you are around her, you have to hold your hands behind your back for fear that you might snatch her baldheaded!

You know your Testy. This is the person God continually uses to test your love. God allows these people so He can work out what is self-centered in us because it takes everything in us to love them.

I picture Testy as someone we would never be around by choice, but the situation has chosen us. Testy is somebody you have to be around a lot. If you're just around someone occasionally, that person really doesn't test you all that much, but Testy has been known to get on your last nerve.

Our challenge is to learn to love Testy. Remember, loving well means that we have been called to do something we are incapable of doing.

What things drive you crazy about Testy? Don't use names—just examples of things Testy has done to irritate you.

Why do you suppose God chose your particular Testy for you?

....
....
....
....
....
....
....

What can you do to minister to your Testy?

....
....
....
....
....
....
....
....
....
....
....

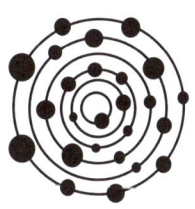 **PRAYER** Lord, You know who Testy is in my life. The scary thing is that I may be Testy in someone else's life. Forgive me and show me how to love the testy people in my life.

FOE

Drawing from the Well

"I tell you who hear me: Love your enemies, do good to those who hate you, bless those who curse you, pray for those who mistreat you." *Luke 6:27-28, NIV*

As Christ's followers, we have been called to love our enemies. If I may be so bold as to ask you a few personal questions: Whom do you hate? Who makes your blood boil? Who are you absolutely not going to forgive to the death? Who has done you so wrong that he or she falls under the category of an enemy to your soul? This is the person we call *Foe.*

It is hard to admit that we hate someone. Chances are this is someone who has been very close to you. I would dare say you do not hate anyone who has not been close enough to hurt you. So you don't have to look far. Foe is somebody with a tremendous amount of access or you would not be in a state of emotional upheaval.

Admit it or not, we've all had them. It's time we were just honest before the Lord and tell Him how we really feel.

Some years ago I struggled with someone that I had to finally admit to the Lord, "I think I hate this person." Maybe you never want to be that ugly, but I thought, *I might as well say it because if I don't, I might never get over it.* I had to ask the Lord not just to heal my heart but also to heal my hatred. Can you relate?

If you can, would you be willing to be honest before the Lord and admit your hatred? Great freedom comes in finally saying the words, "I think I hate this person."

Take some time today to write a letter describing how you feel about Foe. This letter is for your eyes only. Write the good, bad, and ugly, but be honest. After you write out your feelings, ask God to heal you of hatred; then tear up the letter. If you can't think of anyone in your own life that you hate, then you probably know someone else who is struggling with a Foe. Pray for that person to experience healing.

What good things could you pray for your Foe? Please feel no pressure to actually pray those blessings, but do brainstorm and write a list below.

....

....

....

....

....

....

....

....

....

Finally, pray for Foe. Ask only the blessings you can for her. Check off those blessings you have asked, and congratulate yourself for asking at least one blessing for Foe.

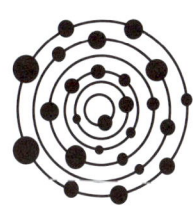

PRAYER Lord, it feels so good to admit that I have harbored hate in my heart. Thank You that Your Word promises forgiveness. "If we confess our sins, He is faithful and righteous to forgive us and cleanse us from all unrighteousness" (1 John 1:9). There is such freedom in honesty.

FAR

Drawing from the Well

"For I was hungry and you gave Me something to eat; I was thirsty and you gave Me something to drink; I was a stranger and you invited Me in; I was naked and you clothed Me; I was sick and you took care of Me; I was in prison and you visited Me. ... And the King will answer them, 'I assure you: Whatever you did for one of the least of these brothers of Mine, you did for Me.'"
Matthew 25:35-36,40

As believers in Christ, we have a biblical mandate to plug into what God is doing across the globe and not just in our personal worlds. We are called to love the stranger, the person who would not even appear on our radar screens unless we allowed God to give us the awareness. It could be the person on the "other side of the tracks," and I mean that no matter which side of the tracks you might be on.

Not only are we called to love the strangers around us, but also we are called to a global perspective. If you and I are to be a people who have a heart like God's, we will be a people who have a heart for the world. We will have to go to them because they will not come to us.

God has not called us to this view just for the needy person but for us as well. Strangers take all sorts of interesting shapes and sizes on any continent or in any city. But we are called to love them because it is an opportunity for us to love with no strings attached, with nothing we can get back from them.

When was the last time you reached out and ministered to a stranger? If it's been a while, look for opportunities close to you such as a homeless shelter, an orphanage, a home for battered women, or someone on the other side of the tracks. Begin where you live, but consider opportunities to be involved in global missions. You can find opportunities available by visiting this Web site: *www.imb.org*

How do you feel when you give with no earthly possibility of being repaid?

_____
_____
_____
_____
_____
_____
_____
_____

List some possibilities you can explore for ministry.

_____
_____
_____
_____
_____
_____
_____
_____
_____

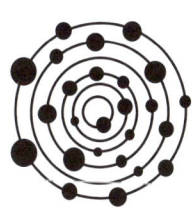 **PRAYER** Lord, I confess that I have been guilty of ignoring strangers. Today You reminded me that You call me to minister to them. Forgive me for my complacency. Help me to do something about it. In Jesus' name.

LETTING GO

Drawing from the Well

"Then Peter came to Him and said, 'Lord, how many times could my brother sin against me and I forgive him? As many as seven times?' 'I tell you, not as many as seven,' Jesus said to him, 'but 70 times seven.'" *Matthew 18:21-22*

A line in the movie *The Diary of a Mad Black Woman* stirred my mind to thinking. In the movie, this lady has been left, forsaken by someone who left her for the proverbial other woman. He manipulated the finances until she had absolutely nothing left. In the movie, she is talking with her mother. The opportunity for revenge has finally come, and it is sweet. You know somewhere along the way your chance for revenge might come also. What do you do?

The mother gives the daughter what I thought to be profound advice when she says, "I know this man put a hurtin' on you, baby, but you've got to forgive him no matter what he does, you've got to forgive him. Not for him, but for you."

The daughter responds with a question, "Forgive him for me?" To which the mother replies, "When somebody hurts you and takes power over you, if you don't forgive them, they keeps the power. Forgive him baby. And after you forgive him, forgive yourself."

The mom is right because when we don't forgive, our offender keeps the power over us. The strangest thing is that our hanging on to unforgiveness keeps it happening over and over and over again. I realized that hanging on to my unforgiveness toward my perpetrator was causing me to be emotionally molested over and over again. But it would not end until I forsook it through forgiveness.

Week Three • Loving People

How do you feel about forgiving someone who has hurt you most?

What do you stand to lose if you do not forgive?

What might you gain by forgiving?

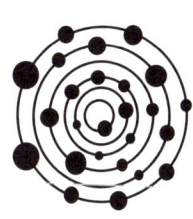

PRAYER Lord, I confess I have harbored anger, bitterness, and unforgiveness far too long. My desire is to be free. Give me the strength to do the hard thing and let go. Thank You for sending Jesus to be the atoning sacrifice for my sins.

6

WEEK
IN REVIEW

This week we have focused on different types of people in our lives that we either love or are challenged to love. List below the four types of people we mentioned.

....

....

....

....

What are some truths that you learned from God's Word about loving different types of people?

....

....

....

....

....

....

....

....

....

....

....

....

Week Three • Loving People

Which type person do you find the most difficult to love?

Write a prayer below asking God to help you love those people in your life whom you find difficult to love.

7

WEEK IN REVIEW

What are some practical ways that you can express love this week to the people in your life who are Joy, Testy, Foe, and Far?

JOY

....

....

....

....

....

....

....

TESTY

....

....

....

....

....

....

....

Week Three • Loving People

FOE

FAR

PRAYER Father, I want to love well the people in my life. Help me not just to think of ways to express my love but also to take those ideas and put them into action this week. Thank You that through the power of the Holy Spirit, I can love others well.

ABIDING IN GOD'S LOVE

Drawing from the Well

"We know that we live in him and he in us because he has given us his Spirit." *1 John 4:13*

"As the Father has loved me, so I have loved you. Now remain in my love." *John 15:9*

What command did Jesus give in John 15:9?

The Greek word used for *abide*, *dwell*, and *remain* are all the same word that is used in 1 John 4:13 for "live." In other words, we are to dwell in God's love. Remember, God can't love us at times and not love us at others. He is love. What He is saying is this, "For you to do what I've called you to do, to be what I've called you to be, to love who I've called you to love, you're going to need to live in a constant awareness of My love for you.

Why is it critical for us to learn to dwell in God's love? Because if we are going to learn to deal with difficult (testy) and impossible (foe) people, we are going to need something that only comes from God. We are incapable of loving well on our own.

Remember 1 John 4:19? "We love because He first loved us." Let's start loving because we're loved, not so we can be loved.

What are some ways you can dwell in God's love?

Week Four • Loving Well

How does loving because we're loved differ from the world's usual approach?

_____

_____

_____

_____

_____

_____

_____

What benefits come from abiding in Christ's love?

_____

_____

_____

_____

_____

_____

_____

_____

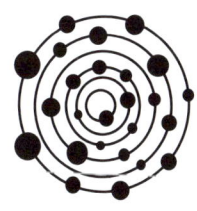 **PRAYER** Lord, because You first loved me, I long to abide in Your love. There is no way I can love difficult and impossible people without a constant awareness of Your love for me. Thank You that I can.

PERFECT LOVE IN MY IMPERFECT HEART

Drawing from the Well

"This hope does not disappoint, because God's love has been poured out in our hearts through the Holy Spirit who was given to us." *Romans 5:5*

Romans 5:5 forms the basis for our third confession: *God pours His perfect love into my imperfect heart.* Isn't it comforting to know when we face Testy and Foe that we don't pull from our own resources to love? The only way we can love them is through the very love God has poured into our hearts by way of the Holy Spirit.

Romans 5:5 in The Message says, "We can't round up enough containers to hold everything God generously pours into our lives through the Holy Spirit!" Each day in Angola we faced lines of people as far as the eye could see, and each person was holding some kind of little cup or bowl. They were standing in line to receive porridge for their one meal a day. Many of the people we fed were children and nursing mothers. Tragically, some stood in line and never got fed.

I thought about all those containers—at the end of it, they would just be piled up. We would come to an end of the porridge, but there's no end to the love of God. So when you have to face Testy again, grab more containers.

How does it make you feel to know that God's love has no end?

Week Four • Loving Well

How has pulling from God's resources made it possible to love when you would not have been able on your own?

What lessons can you pull from the need for a daily infilling?

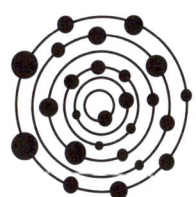

DIFFICULTY: CHOSEN FOR US

Drawing from the Well

"I pray that you, being rooted and firmly established in love, may be able to comprehend with all the saints what is the length and width, height and depth of God's love, and to know the Messiah's love that surpasses knowledge, so you may be filled with all the fullness of God." Ephesians 3:17-19

Today I want us to think about something difficult to accept. The people who drive us crazy have been chosen for us. They have been assigned to us. Isn't that upsetting? In fact, it's not just upsetting. It's just downright hateful, isn't it? Not really. You see, God uses them to complete something lacking in us. If we never learn to allow the character of Christ and His love to flow through us to those persons, then they were placed in our lives for nothing but pain and no gain. Strangely enough, those persons were placed in our lives to bring us gain.

We have difficulty understanding why the people who bring out the worst in us were put there for a reason. They were put in our lives to bring out the worst in us! You see, the more we allow God's love to pour out of us, the closer we come to the day when we will not bite the bait! Then we can see the work of God being done in and through us, and that is the goal. When He does His work, then we are "filled with all the fullness of God."

How does Testy expand your understanding
of Romans 8:28?

_____

_____

_____

_____

_____

Week Four • Loving Well

In what areas of your life do you see God working?

_____

_____

_____

_____

_____

_____

_____

_____

Who in your life drives you crazy? Without naming them, would you write a prayer asking God to give you the endurance needed to let Him complete His work in you?

_____

_____

_____

_____

_____

_____

_____

 **PRAYER** Lord, thank You for stretching me. Even when it hurts, I know You work things for my good.

ABOUNDING LOVE

Drawing from the Well

"This is my prayer: that your love may abound more and more in knowledge and depth of insight." Philippians 1:9, NIV

God wants us to become more and more loving. He has called us to love more than we are and more than we can. How does Philippians 1:9 say our love is to abound? The Bible never encourages us to love blindly. The world says love is blind. God says, "If you want to get yourself in a whole lot of trouble, just let your love be blind!"

God calls us to a love that knows and a heart that is smart. He calls us to love with insight. This is so important because our testy people and our foe both have something broken. If we will let Him, God can give us a heart of compassion and love for them that we did not think possible. Possibly something is broken in both them and us. By the time we really hate someone, something's broken in us. We need insight to see what's broken in both of us. If God gives insight into the other person, we can have compassion.

Think about Testy and Foe in your life. What do you know about them that would give you insight into why they may act like they do?

Week Four • Loving Well

How can the insight you have help you to show love and compassion to them?

....

....

....

....

....

....

....

....

What might God be using them to accomplish in your life?

....

....

....

....

....

....

....

....

....

....

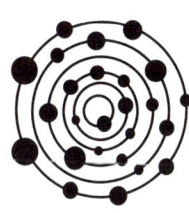

PRAYER God, grant me insight into the lives of those I find testy or my foe. If there is something broken in them or me, help me to have compassion. I want to love them well.

IMITATORS OF GOD

Drawing from the Well

"Be imitators of God, therefore, as dearly loved children and live a life of love, just as Christ loved us and gave himself up for us as a fragrant offering and sacrifice to God." *Ephesians 5:1-2, NIV*

Remember 1 John 4:10, "This is love, not that we loved God, but that he loved us and sent his Son as an atoning sacrifice for our sins." Now, how do we respond in Christ's likeness based on Ephesians 5:1-2, our verses for today?

We imitate Christ in our relationships. Did you notice that Jesus gave Himself as a fragrant offering and sacrifice to God? Beloved, this is crucial: We must forgive. Any anger and bitterness that has taken root in our lives, we must bring to the altar as a gift. As you do, know that it is not so much for others as it is for you. Confess that to the Lord. "Lord, I'm going to tell You that I'm not doing this for them so much as I am for me. I sacrifice what I feel are my rights in this situation, all the things I would really like to say and the grudge I would like to hold. I lay it down, and I forgive instead." Can you do that? In the strength and the power of the Holy Spirit, you can. I did not say it would be easy, but it can be done.

What benefits have you reaped from a past occasion when you forgave?

Why do you think we require the strength and power of the Holy Spirit to sacrifice our most cherished bitterness?

Are you holding on to anything that needs to be placed on the altar? Do you need to forgive someone? Write out what you know you need to do below.

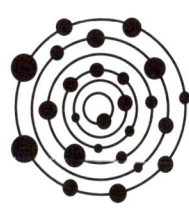

WEEK
IN REVIEW

This week we have focused on loving well. What are some truths you have learned from God's Word about loving well?

What did Jesus mean when He said, "Remain in my love" in John 15:9?

What is the only way we can love others well?

What insight did you learn this week about loving well that you had never considered?

Write a prayer that expresses your heart about loving others well.

WEEK
IN REVIEW

As you flip back through the pages of this journal, write some of the verses below that were most meaningful to you.

What changes have you made in the way that you love people as a result of what you have learned in Loving Well?

What relationships have you seen reconciled since you began to love others well?

....
....
....
....
....

Do other relationships in your life need to be restored?

....
....
....
....
....

What will you do this week to demonstrate God's love to those people?

....
....
....
....

PRAYER Thank You, Lord, that my eyes have been opened to what it means to love others well. I know I can't love in my own strength, but through the power of Your Holy Spirit, I can do all things. Help me never to forget that I cannot give out what I have not taken in. Thank You for loving me well. Help me to imitate You in the way I love others.